FUN WITH SIMPLE SCIENCE

Growing Plants

BARBARA TAYLOR

Kingfisher Books

In this book, you can discover how to grow plants from cuttings, seeds and bulbs and how the environment affects plant growth.

The book is divided into six different topics. Look out for the big headings with a circle at each end – like the one at the top of this page. These headings tell you where a new topic starts.

Pages 4–17

Growing New Plants

Bulbs and tubers; stem and leaf cuttings; sprouting seeds; seed dispersal; spores from mosses, mushrooms, ferns and lichens.

Pages 18–26

Water, Light, Air, Warmth

Seeds and water; roots and water; water pipes inside plants; cacti, bottle gardens, growing towards the light; water plants; seasons.

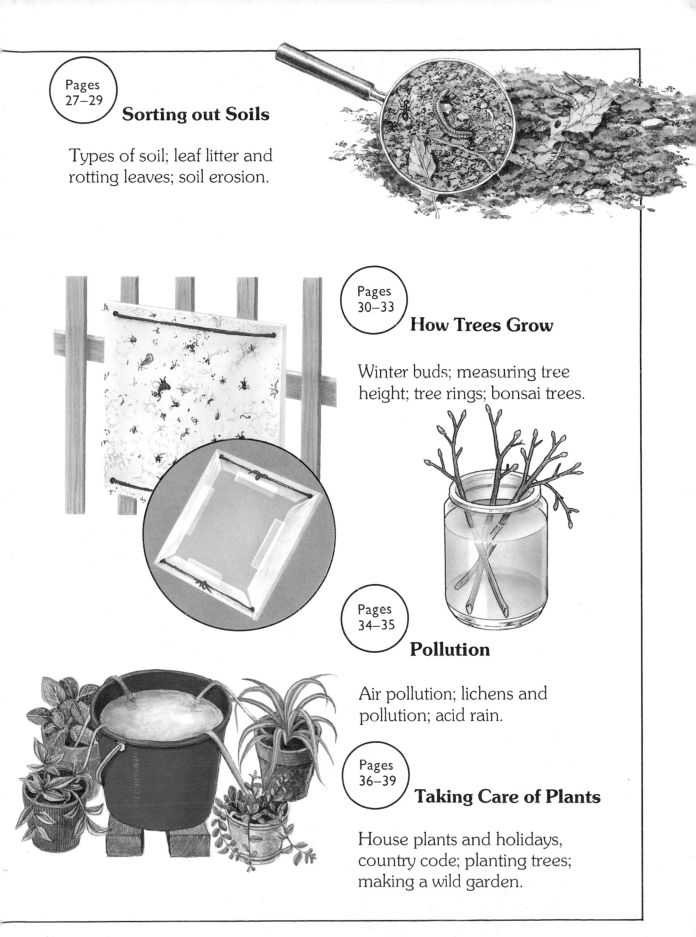

GROWING NEW PLANTS

Have you ever grown a carrot top? If you put the top of a carrot in a saucer of water, it will sprout leaves. The leaves use the food stored in the carrot to grow. How long does it take for the leaves to appear?

You could also grow tops of other fruits or vegetables, such as pineapples, parsnips or turnips. How are they different from the carrot?

Pineapple top

▼ How many different kinds of bulb flowers can you see in this picture? As each new bulb is exactly the same as its parent, people can grow lots of bulbs which are exactly the same.

Seeds, Bulbs and Cuttings

There are lots of different ways to grow plants. Here are the three main ways.

We can grow some new plants from seeds, which are produced in flowers. Each seed may grow into a new plant that is different from its parent plant.

Seeds

Some plants grow long, spindly stems and sprout new plants at intervals along the stem. These new plants are identical to their parent plants.

Runner

Other new plants grow from pieces of old plants, such as bulbs or cuttings of stems or leaves. These new plants are also identical to their parent plants.

Bulb

Cutting

Looking Inside Bulbs

A bulb is an underground stem. It is made up of a flattened stem and a bud surrounded by short swollen leaves. The leaves are full of stored food. In winter, leaves above the ground turn brown and die. Next spring new leaves grow using the food stored in the bulb.

Onion

Daffodil

Tulip

Bulb cut in half

Swollen leaves

Bud

Growing Bulbs

If you grow a bulb such as a hyacinth in water, you will be able to watch the roots develop.

1. Find a jar with a thin neck and fill it with water almost up to the neck. Place the bulb in the neck of the jar.
2. Place the jar in a cool, dark place until you can see a shoot pushing out of the top of the bulb and the roots are about 10 centimetres long.
3. Move the bulb to a warm, light place to finish growing. Make sure the jar is always full of water. How long does it take for the shoot to appear? How long do the roots grow?

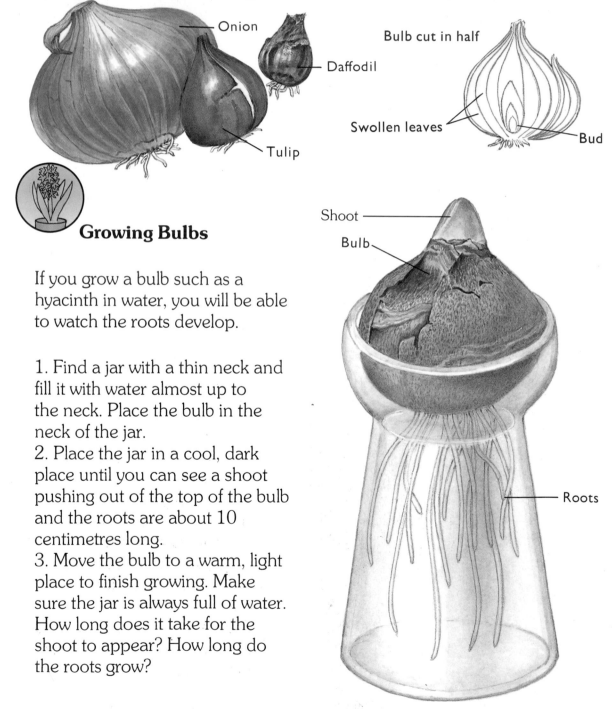

Shoot

Bulb

Roots

Potting Potatoes

Like bulbs, potatoes are a kind of underground stem. They are called tubers. Tubers store food both to produce new plants and to help the plant survive underground when conditions are not good for growing. The 'eyes' of a potato are really buds, which will sprout into shoots and grow leaves. You can grow several new plants from one potato.

Potato

Cocktail stick

1. Push four cocktail sticks into one end of a potato.
2. Balance the potato over a glass jar full of water. Keep the jar topped up with water.
3. In a few days, shoots will grow from the eyes. Take the potato out of the water and ask an adult to help you cut out each shoot, with a little piece of potato behind it.
4. Plant each shoot in a separate plant pot, covering with soil or potting compost.

Growing Bits of Plants

You will need:

lots of containers (such as old yogurt pots, plastic bottles or mugs, old egg boxes or food trays), soil or potting compost, thin sticks, a trowel, labels, notebook and pencil, plastic bags, elastic bands, scissors, cuttings from different plants (see below).

Plastic bags

Cup

Yogurt pot

Small stick

Labels

Spoon

Pen

How to Take Stem Cuttings

Cut off the tips of side shoots or young stems without flowers in the summer months. This is when plants do most of their growing. Ask an adult to help you make a clean cut just below a leaf node with a pair of scissors or a sharp knife. Make the cuttings about 8–10 centimetres long and strip off the lower leaves. Stand the cuttings in a container of water until they grow roots, then plant them in soil or compost.

Cactus

Geranium cutting

You can also plant offsets which sprout from bigger plants

Spider plant

Place each cutting carefully in a hole.

Water the soil or compost well.

Cover each container with a plastic bag.

1. Make some holes in the bottom of your containers and put a few small stones in the bottom. This helps water to drain away so the soil will not get waterlogged.

2. Fill each container with soil or potting compost.

3. Use the stick to make one or more holes in the soil.

4. Place one cutting carefully in each hole, taking care not to bend or crush the cutting.

5. Put a little more soil around the cuttings. Press the soil down firmly so that the cuttings stand upright.

6. Over a sink or outside, fill the container to the brim with water and let the water drain through.

7. Cover each container with a plastic bag and hold the bag in place with an elastic band (see page 21).

8. After a few days, take off the bag. Keep the soil warm and damp.

9. The cuttings should eventually grow roots and new leaves, but be patient – this won't happen overnight! When some new leaves have grown, transplant each cutting into its own container.

What happens

When you take a cutting from a plant, it can grow new roots and leaves to survive on its own. The parent plant may also sprout new shoots and leaves to replace those you cut off. This is possible because plants (unlike animals) grow all through their lives. Growth is concentrated in certain areas, such as the tips of roots and shoots.

Loads More Leaves

Plants with thick, hairy or fleshy leaves can be grown from leaf cuttings. The best time to take leaf cuttings is from June to September. You will need the same materials as for stem cuttings (see page 8). Plant several leaf cuttings in a pot of damp soil or potting compost. Cover the pot with a plastic bag to keep the air around the cuttings moist. Look at page 20 to see how this works. When the cuttings have sprouted new leaves, separate them carefully, without breaking the roots if possible. Move each cutting to its own pot and leave it in a warm, shady place for a few weeks until it is growing well. How long do your cuttings take to sprout new leaves?

Jade Plants

Jade plants can be grown from just one leaf. Carefully pull a few leaves off a plant and leave them to dry. Then plant the leaves so they just stand up in the soil or compost. They should grow new shoots in a couple of weeks.

African Violets

African violets will also grow from leaves. Ask an adult to help you cut a young, healthy leaf off the plant. Make sure it is a clean cut with some leaf stalk attached. When you plant the stalk, keep the leaf itself clear of the soil.

Jade plant

African violet

1. Cut main veins under the leaf

2. Weight the leaf down with pebbles

3. New plants sprout from cuts

A New Begonia

With a big enough leaf, you can grow several new plants from one leaf. Begonias can be grown like this. Choose a large, healthy leaf and cut it off the plant. Ask an adult to help you make cuts underneath the leaf on the main veins. Lay the leaf on top of the soil or potting compost with the cut side down. Weight the leaf with some pebbles to keep it near the soil and watch what happens.

How many new plants can you grow from one leaf? How long do they take to grow? Place your cuttings in different places around the room. Does this make any difference to how they grow?

Sorting Seeds

Go on a seed hunt in gardens, hedges, woods and waste ground to make your own collection of seeds. You will also find some seeds in wild bird food or pet food. Do not forget the seeds we eat, such as rice, maize or corn, oats, nuts, beans and peas, nor the seeds inside fruits, such as peaches or apples. How are your seeds the same? How are they different? See how many ways you can find to sort your collection into groups. Here are some ideas: size, weight, wild seeds, seeds from trees or seeds from the farm.

Can you make a picture of some of the different groups of seeds in your collection? Stick the seeds on to coloured card.

As well as measuring seeds with a ruler, you could also see how many will fit into an egg cup or a square 10 centimetres by 10 centimetres.

Small seeds

Mosses, Ferns and Lichens

Mosses, ferns, lichens and fungi do not have flowers so they cannot make seeds. Instead they produce spores, which are very small, simple structures. A spore usually consists of one cell and does not have a

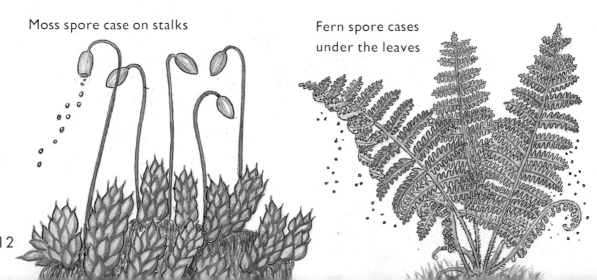

Moss spore case on stalks

Fern spore cases under the leaves

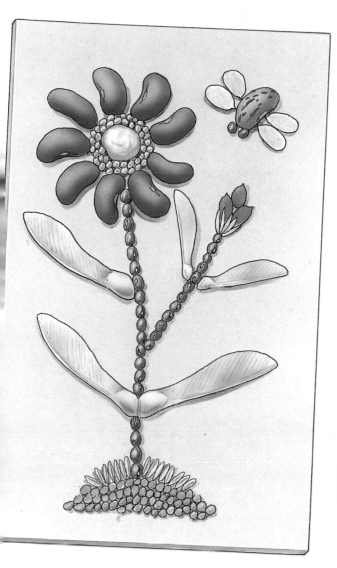

Mushroom Patterns

The spores of the mushrooms we eat are produced under the cap. To make a spore print, cut off the cap and lay it down on some white paper. Cover the mushroom with a box or a jar to keep out the draughts and leave it overnight. The pattern you will see the next day is made by the spores which fall off the cap.

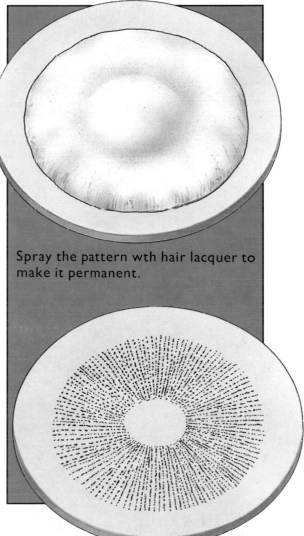

Spray the pattern wth hair lacquer to make it permanent.

store of food. If a spore lands in a suitable place, it may grow into a new plant.

◀ Lichen spores may be in discs, cups or spheres

13

Seeds on the Move

Have you ever noticed all the little seedlings growing under a tree? If seeds sprout too close to their parent plant, they will not have enough space, light or water to grow. They stand a better chance of growing and surviving if they move further away.

Some plants have special ways of shooting out their seeds so they land some way away. Squirting cucumber seeds can end up eight metres away from their parent plant. But most seeds rely on the wind, water or animals to move them to a new home.

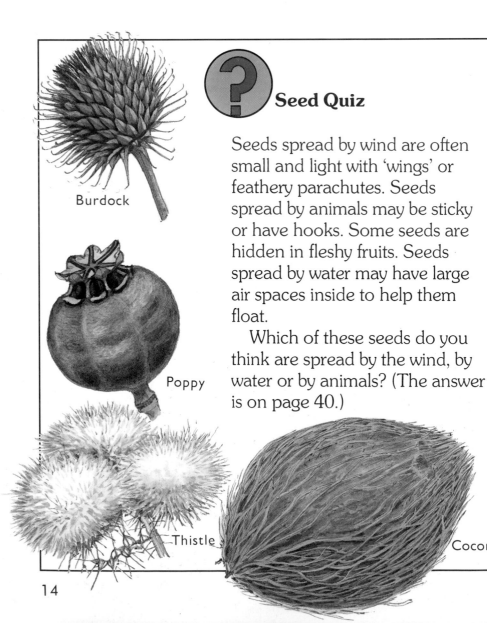

? Seed Quiz

Seeds spread by wind are often small and light with 'wings' or feathery parachutes. Seeds spread by animals may be sticky or have hooks. Some seeds are hidden in fleshy fruits. Seeds spread by water may have large air spaces inside to help them float.

Which of these seeds do you think are spread by the wind, by water or by animals? (The answer is on page 40.)

Burdock

Poppy

Thistle

Coconut

Willowherb

Nut

Blackberry

▲ Some plants hide their seeds inside tasty berries to encourage animals or birds to eat them. These seeds pass through an animal's insides unharmed and grow into new plants.

 Grow an Avocado Tree

You can grow unusual house plants from avocados or dates.

1. Stick toothpicks into the side of an avocado stone. This encourages the roots to grow.
2. Balance the stone over a jar of water so that it is just touching the level of the water.
3. When some short roots have grown, take the stone out of the jar and plant it in a container of soil or potting compost (see pages 8 and 9).

Avocado

Which way is up?

1. Soak some fresh bean seeds in water overnight.
2. Cut a piece of blotting paper to fit around the insides of two large jars with wide necks.
3. Push crumpled paper towels into the middle of the jars.
4. Push a few soaked seeds between the blotting paper and the side of the jar. Place the seeds in different positions – vertical, horizontal and at an angle.
5. Keep the jars in a warm place out of direct sunlight. Water the paper towels regularly to keep the blotting paper moist.
6. After a few days, roots and shoots will start to appear. This is called germination. Which grows first – the roots or the shoots? Which direction do the roots and shoots grow in?
7. When the roots and shoots are a few centimetres long, turn one of the jars upside down. What happens?

What happens
Roots usually grow down because they are attracted by the pull of the Earth's gravity. This strong, invisible force pulls everything towards the middle of the Earth. The shoots always grow upwards towards the light.

Investigating Seeds

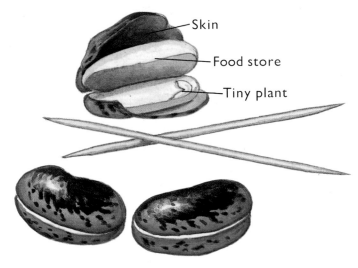

Skin

Food store

Tiny plant

Use cocktail sticks to take some different seeds, such as beans, peas or wheat, apart. First peel off the seed skin, called the testa. The testa is a tough waterproof coat which protects the seed. Water gets into the seed through a tiny hole in the testa called the micropyle.

Inside the testa, you should be able to see a tiny plant and one or two seed leaves. A broad bean has two large seed leaves. Which other seeds have two seed leaves? Can you find any seeds with one seed leaf? Sometimes, the seed leaves contain stored food.

Growing Seeds

See if you can measure and compare the growth of different seeds. Cress seeds grow quickly, but runner bean seeds are bigger and easier to measure. Take one of the seeds out every day and measure the roots, shoots and leaves. Mark the edge of a leaf or the tip of a root so you can see where most of the growing is taking place. Do the plants grow all over or just at the edges?

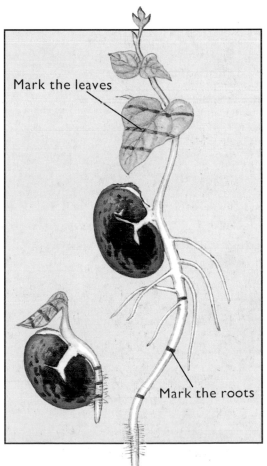

Mark the leaves

Mark the roots

How does the environment around a plant affect the way it grows? Four of the most important factors are water, light, air and temperature. To investigate water, make four equal groups of cress seeds and soak three overnight.

 **Plants and Water**

Seeds

1

2

Covers

3

4

1. In the first container, put some wet seeds on wet cotton wool.
2. In the second container, put wet seeds on dry cotton wool.
3. In the third container, put another group of wet seeds on top of dry cotton wool. Cover the seeds and cotton wool with water. Keep these seeds and those in the first container damp.
4. In the last container, put the dry seeds on top of dry cotton wool. Cover all containers and leave for a few days.

What happens

Seeds need the right amount of water to germinate properly. Dry seeds on dry cotton wool will not grow at all. Wet seeds on dry cotton wool will shrivel up and die. Seeds under water will go rotten. Only wet seeds on wet cotton wool grow well.

Make a clown from modelling clay, leaving a dip in its head. Put damp cress seeds on damp cotton wool in the dip. Watch the clown's hair grow.

Roots and Water

1. Place a clay flower pot full of water in a large bowl.
2. Pack a mixture of soil and sawdust around the pot.
3. Put some soaked peas on the surface of the soil.
4. After a few days, brush the soil off the peas. In which direction are the roots growing?

Flowerpot

Peas

Bowl

What happens

When the only source of water is in the flower pot, the roots grow sideways towards the water. Water is so important to the seeds that the need for water overcomes the pull of gravity.

▼ Rice is planted in fields which are flooded with water. These are called paddy fields. Rice grows well with its roots in lots of water and its shoots in the air.

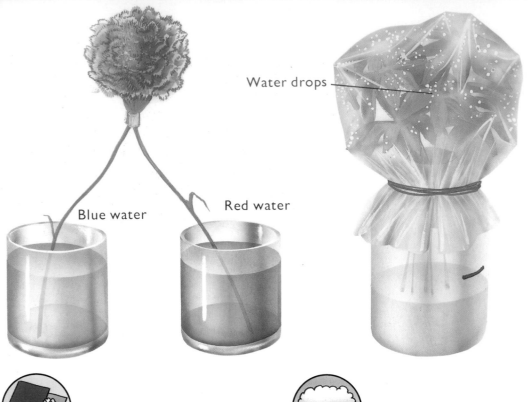

Blue water

Red water

Water drops

Make a Blue and Red Flower

1. Fill one of two clean containers with blue food colouring.
2. Fill the other container with red food colouring.
3. Carefully split the stem of a white carnation from the bottom to the top. Put one half of the stem in the blue water and the other half in the red water.
4. After several hours, some of the petals will turn blue and some will turn red. How long does your flower take to change colour?

What happens
The carnation 'drinks' the coloured water through thin pipes in its stem into the petals.

Giving off Water

1. Fill a large plastic bottle with water and mark the water level.
2. Place a plant in the water and seal the neck of the bottle.
3. Put a plastic bag over the leaves and fix it to the bottle.
4. Leave the plant in the sun for a few days. What happens to the water level? Can you see droplets of moisture on the bag?

What happens
The plant takes up some of the water through its roots. So the water level in the bottle goes down. This water travels up the pipes in the stem and passes out through tiny holes in the leaves.

▲ Cacti have spines instead of leaves, so they do not give off as much water. Spines also collect morning dew and help to shade the plant from hot sun. Animals find it hard to drink water from a plant with spiny prickles. The stems of many cacti, such as saguaros, can expand like a concertina to store water. Their roots spread out in a wide, shallow network to catch as much water as possible when it does rain.

Make a Bottle Garden

Bottle gardens are simple and fun to make and a very good way to watch plants grow.

You will need:
a large glass or plastic container with a top, gravel, charcoal, potting compost, a funnel, long sticks, a stick with a cotton reel fixed to the end, a plastic spoon or fork tied to the end of a garden cane, a sponge on the end of a stick, small, slow-growing plants such as ferns and mosses.

1. Use the sponge on a stick to clean and dry the container.
2. Put the funnel into the neck of the bottle and pour in a layer of gravel, then some crushed charcoal and finally dry potting compost.
3. Moisten the compost and pack it down firmly inside the bottle with the cotton reel on a stick.
4. Use the fork or spoon on a cane to make some small holes in the potting compost.
5. Use the thin sticks to lower in each plant carefully on to the soil.
6. Put the top on the bottle to seal any moisture inside.
7. Stand the bottle in a bright corner out of direct sunlight. After a day or so, can you see drops of moisture forming on the sides of the bottle?
8. After a few months, take the top off the bottle to refresh the air and add a little water if necessary.

If you grow plants in a sealed bottle, they will give off water which will run down the sides of the bottle into the soil. This water can be taken up by the plant again. If the water balance is right, you will not need to water your bottle garden for several months.

 **Follow the Sun**

Did you know that some plants, such as sunflowers, turn to face the Sun as it moves across the sky? Plants use the energy in light to make their food. A green pigment called chlorophyll traps the Sun's energy. Plants are the only living things that can make their own food. All animals have to eat plants – or animals that have eaten plants.

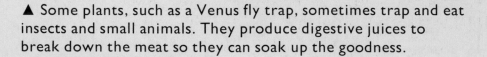
▲ Some plants, such as a Venus fly trap, sometimes trap and eat insects and small animals. They produce digestive juices to break down the meat so they can soak up the goodness.

Make a Potato Maze

1. Make a small hole in a short side of a long cardboard box.
2. Cut out several pieces of cardboard and stick them inside the box to make a maze like the one in the picture.
3. Put a sprouting potato at the end of the box opposite the hole and place the lid on the box.
4. Leave the box in a light place so that light can easily get into the box through the hole in the end.
5. After a few days, take the lid off the box. Has your potato found the pathway through the 'maze' to reach the light?

What happens

The potato senses the light and grows towards it, even though it has to find its way through a maze first. Does your potato shoot eventually grow out of the hole in the side of the box?

Airy Plants

Air is very important to plants. Can you think why we put water weeds in a fish tank?

Cut a short length of pondweed and leave it in a jar on a sunny window-sill. Look carefully at the leaves. Can you see any bubbles in the water? When plants make food, they also give off a gas called oxygen. The bubbles given off by the pondweed are bubbles of oxygen. This is the gas that plants and animals, including fishes, need to breathe to stay alive.

Air bubbles

Hot and Cold Plants

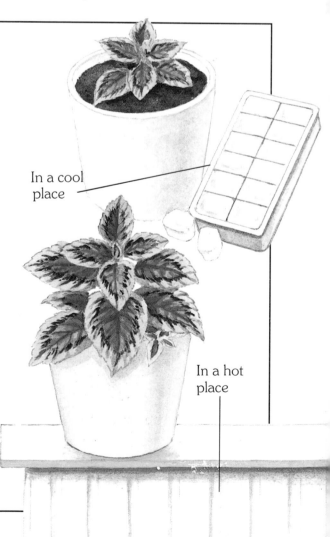

In a cool place

In a hot place

Keep two similar seedlings at different temperatures to see how this affects their growth. Put one in a warm place and one in a cold place. Make sure both seedlings have the same amount of light so they can make food.

Some seeds, such as apple seeds, need a cold period before they will sprout. In the natural world, this means seeds shed in autumn will not grow until warmer weather returns in spring.

Put apple pips in the refrigerator for a few days before planting.

SORTING OUT SOILS

Plants need water and minerals from the soil in order to grow well. There are lots of different kinds of soil, such as clay soil, sandy soil or chalky soil. Some plants only grow well in certain types of soil.

Clay soils hold water and often become waterlogged. In sandy soils, water quickly drains away. In winter, the water in the soil is frozen. Trees with wide, flat leaves cannot draw up enough water to replace that lost from their leaves. So they drop their leaves and rest over the winter.

Collect some soils and see how many differences you can find. What is the texture like? Is the soil smooth, sticky or gritty? Look at the soil carefully with a magnifying glass.

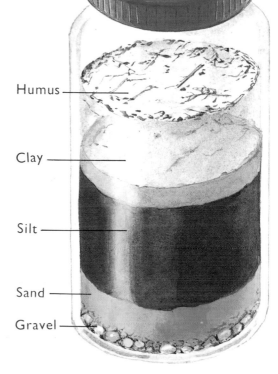

Separating Soil

Make the soil separate by shaking some up in a jar of water and leaving it to soak for a day or two. How many layers can you see? How big are the pieces on the bottom? Are there any bits floating on the surface? Try this investigation again with different kinds of soil.

Humus

Clay

Silt

Sand

Gravel

Rotten Old Leaves

In autumn, look at the rotting leaves under the trees in a wood, a park or a garden. This is called leaf litter. Use a magnifying glass to look at the leaves. How are they different from the leaves on a tree? Can you find any leaf skeletons?

When tree leaves fall to the ground, they are gradually broken into pieces as fungi, bacteria and minibeasts such as worms feed on the leaves. The breakdown of leaves, called decomposition, brings the goodness in the leaves back into the soil to make it rich. Plants can take up the nutrients in the soil and use them to grow.

How Long do Leaves take to Rot?

Collect some leaves from different kinds of tree. Bury the leaves under the soil in a container. Label each leaf and keep the soil moist. Every two weeks dig up the leaves to see how much they have rotted away. You may see fungi feeding as a mass of white threads. Then bury the leaves again. Do some leaves decompose faster than others? Some may take years to rot completely and turn into crumbs. But you can watch the start of the rotting process.

Disappearing Soil

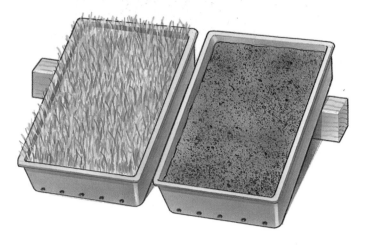

1. Ask an adult to make holes in one end of two seed trays.
2. Fill both trays with soil.
3. Plant grass seeds in one tray. Leave the soil in the other bare.
4. When the grass has grown a few centimetres high, prop the trays up on two blocks of wood, so they are on a slope. Place a bucket below the holes at the end of each tray.
5. Pour the same amount of water, from the same height, into the end of the trays furthest from the holes. How much soil is washed out of each tray?
6. What happens if you make furrows across the tray with bare soil?

▼ Marram grass roots spread in a thick network through the sand. They help to stop sand dunes from being blown away.

Trees grow in two main ways. The twigs and branches grow longer at the tips, so the tree becomes taller and wider. At the same time, the trunk, branches and twigs all grow fatter. Twigs form new buds at the end of the year.

How Old is a Twig?

Look carefully at a tree twig. Can you see little circles or rings around the twig? These are called girdle scars. They mark the spot where the twig starts to grow each year. By counting the girdle scars, you can work out the age of a twig. If you measure the distance between the girdle scars, you can work out how much the twig grew each year.

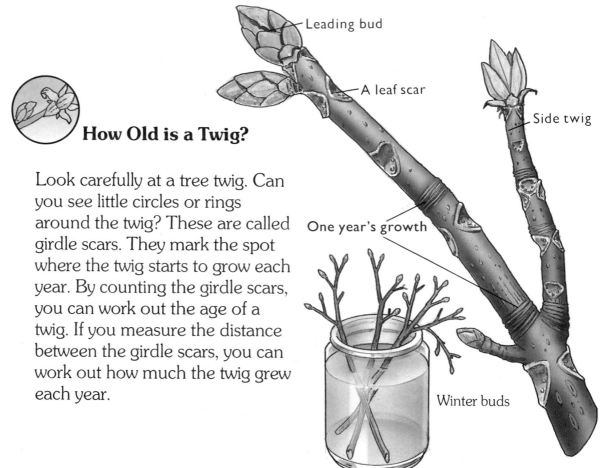

Leading bud

A leaf scar

Side twig

One year's growth

Winter buds

Growing Buds

The winter buds on a tree contain the beginnings of the shoot, leaves and flowers for the following year. The thick, overlapping scales protect the delicate contents of the bud from cold, from insect attack or from drying out. In spring, bring some twigs indoors and leave them in a jar of water in a warm, sunny place. The best trees to try are horse chestnut ('sticky buds'), willow or birch. The buds may take some weeks to open, but you can watch how the leaves unfold and burst out of the scales.

Trees from Twigs

You can grow trees from small pieces of twig. It is better to pull off the twig, rather than cutting it. Take a small piece of the main twig too. Plant the twig upright in soil or potting compost (pages 8 and 9) or leave it in a jar of water until it has grown some roots, and then plant it. Try this with willow, poplar or hawthorn trees.

How Tall is a Tree?

Here is a simple way to measure how high a tree has grown. Hold a stick or pencil in front of you, and walk backwards and forwards until the top and bottom of the stick or pencil are level with the top and bottom of the tree. Turn the pencil on its side and ask a friend to walk away from the tree at right angles to you. Stop them when he or she is level with the end of the pencil. You can then measure the distance between the tree and your friend. This distance will equal the height of the tree.

Did You Know?

The largest living thing on Earth is the General Sherman Sequoi Tree in California. It is 83.8 metres tall, and the trunk weighs approximately 1,256 metric tons. Experts believe that this giant tree is over 2500–3000 years old.

▲ Bonsai trees start off as normal trees but do not get enough food and water to grow to their normal size. They are miniatures, and their shoots and roots are pruned to stunt their growth. Bonsai trees can take hundreds of years to grow. If you keep trimming the leaves and shoots of a tree seedling, giving it only a little room to grow, you can make your own bonsai tree.

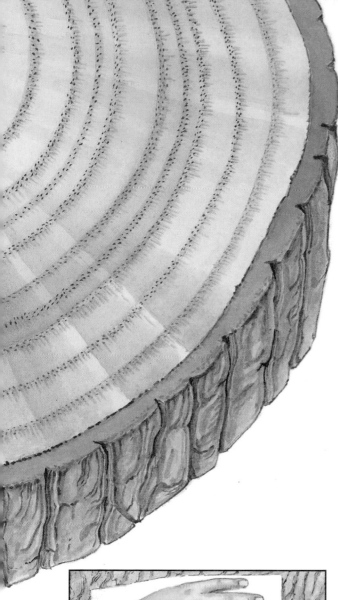

Counting Rings

If you find a tree stump or a pile of cut logs in a plantation, you can work out the age of the trees by counting the rings in the trunk. It is easiest to count the darker rings, showing the end of each year's growth. Measure the width of each ring to see how the amount of growth varies from year to year. If growing conditions are good, the rings will be wider and further apart. Narrow rings show that growth has been slower in those years. Can you think of any reasons why?

Bark Rubbings

The bark of a tree protects it from damage, from drying out or from attack by insects. As the trunk grows, the bark grows, stretches and cracks like skin.

Lay a piece of paper against tree bark and rub over the top with a wax crayon. Don't rub too hard or you will tear the paper. How is the bark of each kind of tree different? How many different kinds of bark can you find? Can you identify trees just by looking at their bark?

POLLUTION

Plants often find it hard to grow because people have polluted the environment with poisonous waste products from homes, cars, factories or farms.

 How Polluted is the Air in your Area?

Make some sticky squares by gluing sticky-backed plastic on to cardboard. Fix them outside in different places. After a few days, look at them with a magnifying glass. How much dirt has each collected? Where are the most polluted places in your area? Where are plants growing best?

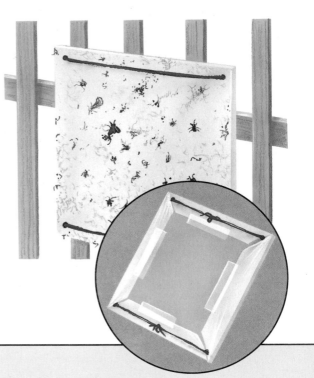

 Looking for Lichens

Plants called lichens don't like pollution, such as acid rain. They have no roots and absorb any poisons in the air or water all over their surface. If the poisons build up, they may eventually kill the lichens. Small, flat lichens can cope with highish levels of pollution. So can crusty orange lichens, which grow mostly on stones. But leafy, bushy lichens can survive only in really clean air.

Go on a lichen hunt in your area. Look on walls, roofs, gravestones and tree trunks. Which sort of lichens can you find? The type of lichen will give you a clue to the amount of pollution in your area. If the air is very polluted, you will not find any lichens at all.

▲ Acid rain is formed when poisonous gases from power stations, factories and vehicle exhausts mix with water in the air. Acid rain damages plant growth and weakens the plant. Trees with needles are most likely to be affected.

Medium pollution
Grey-green crusty lichens

Medium pollution
Orange crusty lichens

Clean air
Bushy, feathery lichens

Different kinds of plants need different growing conditions. Some plants hate direct sunlight while others grow well in it. Too much water is just as bad for house plants as too little water (see page 18). A good watering once a week is usually better than a few drops every day. House plants need more water in spring and summer.

 House Plants and Holidays

When you go on holiday, move your house plants out of the sun and take off any flowers. They use up a lot of water. Here are three ideas for watering your plants while you are away on holiday. Can you think of some more ways?

1. Cover the plant pots with a plastic bag held in place with an elastic band. (See page 20).
2. Put several plants in pots in a large bowl of wet newspaper, potting compost or just water. The plants will gradually soak up water through the holes in the bottom of the pots.
3. Fill a container, such as a bucket or an empty ice-cream tub with water. Arrange several plants around the container, but lower down. Hang some lamp wicks from the water container to touch the soil in each pot. The wicks will gradually soak up the water and carry it down to the soil in each pot. The thickness of the wick controls the speed at which the water moves.

▲ All over the world, too many trees are being cut down and not enough planted to take their place. See if you can help to plant more trees in your area. You can also recycle more paper instead of throwing it away. Every tonne of paper that is recycled can save 17 trees.

Country Walks

If you go for a walk in the countryside, be careful not to damage the plants growing there. Remember these points:

✳ Keep to paths and avoid trampling on plants.
✳ Do not pick wild plants. Take photographs or make sketches instead.
✳ Make sure the adults you are with take care with matches, campfires or barbecues. Dry plants catch light easily and fires are hard to put out.
✳ Take litter home with you. It can poison the environment and materials such as plastics may not rot away.
✳ Help to keep the water clean. Don't throw things in streams or rivers.

Making a Wild Garden

Ask an adult to help you make a
patch of ground into an area where
wild plants can grow. The plants will attract insects and wildlife.

Let the grass grow long and allow weeds such as thistles and nettles
to grow in small areas. Caterpillars feed on nettles and many insects,
such as grasshoppers, shelter or lay eggs in the grass.

Clear a patch of soil and sow wild flower seeds just under the surface.
Water the soil to keep it moist. Good seeds to plant are: clover,
cornflower, meadowsweet, scabious, poppies, white campion, bird's foot
trefoil and knapweed.

If there is a fence or wall, you can grow climbing plants such as
honeysuckle or ivy. These will attract insects and provide shelter for
snails. Birds may eventually nest in the tangle of leaves and stems.

Ask an adult to help you build a compost heap where minibeasts can
live and which will provide food for birds.

A Window-Box

If you don't have a patch of ground, you can grow wild plants or herbs in a window-box or a large tray. Keep the soil moist, but not waterlogged. It is best to make some drainage holes in the bottom of the container. Take out some of the plants from time to time so the others will have enough space to grow. Before the plants die back in winter, take some cuttings or collect any seeds ready for next year.

INDEX

Answers to quiz on page 14:
Things spread by wind: willowherb, poppy, thistle. Things spread by animals: nut, blackberry, burdock. Things spread by water: coconut.

Adviser: Robert Pressling
Designer: Ben White
Editor: Catherine Bradley
Picture Research: Elaine Willis

The publishers wish to thank the following for kindly supplying photographs for this book:
Page 4 ZEFA; 15 Frank Lane Picture Agency; 19 ZEFA; 21 Nature Photographers; 24 NHPA/Stephen Dalton; 29 NHPA/David Woodfall; 32 Heather Angel/Biofotos; 35 NHPA/Silvestris; 37 Mark Edwards/Still Pictures.

The publishers wish to thank the following artists for contributing to this book:
Peter Bull: page headings; Kuo Kang Chen: cover, pp.12/13, 22/23, 28/29, 30/31; Eleanor Ludgate of Jillian Burgess

Illustrations pp.4/5, 20, 34/35; Josephine Martin of Garden Studio pp.6/7, 14/15, 16/17, 26/27, 32/33, 38/39; Patricia Newell of John Martin & Artists Ltd. pp.8/9, 10/11, 18/19, 24/25, 36/37.

Kingfisher Books, Grieswood and Dempsey Ltd. Elsley House, 24–30 Great Titchfield Street, London W1P 7AD

First published in 1991 by Kingfisher Books

© Griesewood and Dempsey Ltd. 1991

British Library Cataloguing in Publication Data
Taylor, Barbara
  Growing plants.
  1. Plants
  I. Title   II. Series
  581

ISBN 0 86272 751 0

Phototypeset by Southern Positives and Negatives (SPAN), Lingfield, Surrey
Colour separations by Scantrans pte Ltd, Singapore
Printed in Hong Kong